NATIVE
AMERICAN
NATIONS

THE
SENECA

BY BETTY MARCKS

CONSULTANT: TIM TOPPER,
CHEYENNE RIVER SIOUX

BLASTOFF!
DISCOVERY

BELLWETHER MEDIA • MINNEAPOLIS, MN

Author's Statement of Positionality:
I am a white woman of European descent. As such, I can claim no direct lived experience of being a Native American. In writing this book, I have tried to be an ally by relying on sources by Native American writers and authors whenever possible and have worked to let their voices guide its content.

This edition first published in 2026 by Bellwether Media, Inc.

No part of this publication may be reproduced in whole or in part without written permission of the publisher.
For information regarding permission, write to Bellwether Media, Inc.,
Attention: Permissions Department,
3500 American Blvd W, Suite 150, Bloomington, MN 55431.

Library of Congress Cataloging-in-Publication Data

LC record for The Seneca available at: https://lccn.loc.gov/2025018377

Text copyright © 2026 by Bellwether Media, Inc. BLASTOFF! DISCOVERY and associated logos are trademarks and/or registered trademarks of Bellwether Media, Inc. Bellwether Media is a division of FlutterBee Education Group.

Editor: Elizabeth Neuenfeldt   Series Designer: Andrea Schneider
Book Designer: Laura Sowers

Printed in the United States of America, North Mankato, MN.

TABLE OF CONTENTS

GREAT HILL PEOPLE	4
TRADITIONAL SENECA LIFE	6
EUROPEAN CONTACT	12
LIFE TODAY	16
CONTINUING TRADITIONS	20
FIGHT TODAY, BRIGHT TOMORROW	24
TIMELINE	28
GLOSSARY	30
TO LEARN MORE	31
INDEX	32

GREAT HILL PEOPLE

The Seneca are a nation of Native American people. They call themselves *Onöndowa'ga:'*. This means "Great Hill People." The nation is the largest of the Haudenosaunee **Confederacy**. This Confederacy is also called the Iroquois Confederacy or Six Nations.

The Seneca are known as "Keepers of the Western Door." Their homeland is the farthest west of this Confederacy. It spans the Finger Lakes region of Central New York. It also includes the Genesee Valley in Western New York.

SENECA LANDS AROUND 1720

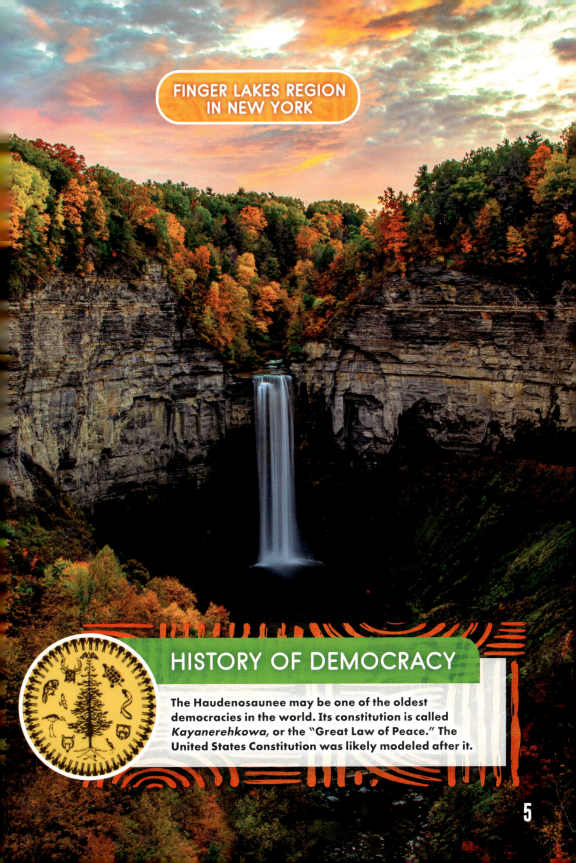

FINGER LAKES REGION IN NEW YORK

HISTORY OF DEMOCRACY

The Haudenosaunee may be one of the oldest democracies in the world. Its constitution is called *Kayanerehkowa,* or the "Great Law of Peace." The United States Constitution was likely modeled after it.

TRADITIONAL SENECA LIFE

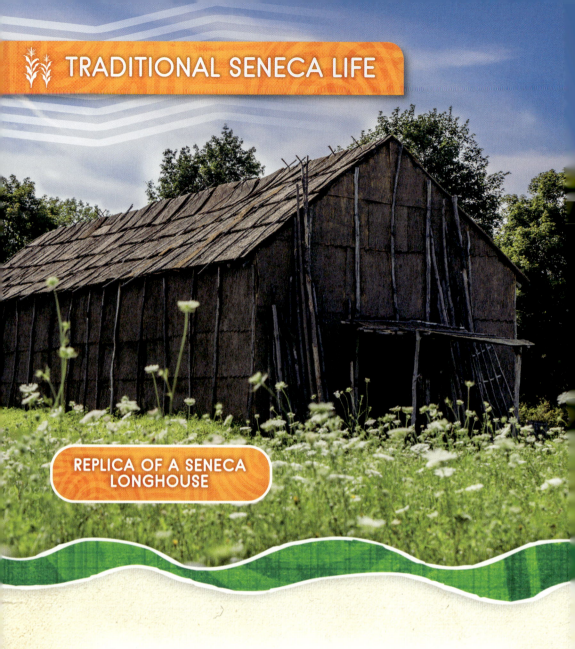

REPLICA OF A SENECA LONGHOUSE

The Seneca practice a **matrilineal clan** system. Animals represent the different clans. All people within a clan are relatives. The Seneca have eight clans. They are the Turtle, Wolf, Heron, Snipe, Hawk, Bear, Deer, and Beaver Clans. A Snipe is a type of bird.

Seneca villages once included longhouses. Each clan within a village had a longhouse. A Clan Mother was the head of the house. All her female **descendants** and their husbands lived in her house. Clan Mothers made important decisions for their clans. Clan members could not marry within their clans.

REPLICA OF THE INSIDE OF A SENECA LONGHOUSE

CORN BRAIDING

Ancestral Seneca lived in cleared woodlands near fresh waterways. They often built tall wooden fences around their villages. Families planted large fields of crops. They grew corn, beans, and squash. These foods were called the Three Sisters. They were known as "the life supporters." People also gathered nuts, berries, and roots.

Ancestral Seneca also hunted and fished. Men hunted in groups. They used bows, arrows, and spears. They mostly hunted deer. All parts of the deer were used. Deer meat provided food. Other parts were used for clothing and tools.

SENECA RESOURCES

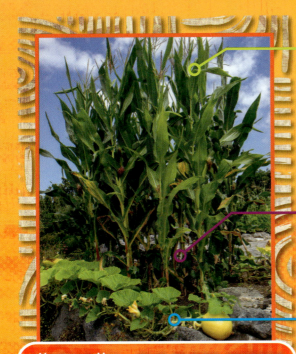

JÖHEHGÖH – THE THREE SISTERS

ONEO' – CORN

OSAE'DA' – BEANS

ONYÖHSA' – SQUASH

The Seneca practice **ceremonies** throughout the year just like their ancestors. The ceremonies honor seasons of the year. They also celebrate the different stages of food growth and harvests. They often include singing, dancing, games, and food.

One of the first ceremonies of the year is the Maple Ceremony. Sap is collected and boiled into syrup. The Thanking the Trees ceremony follows. The Sun Dance occurs each spring. The Strawberry Dance celebrates the return of warm weather. The Green Corn Ceremony honors the year's corn harvest.

PRESENT-DAY SAP COLLECTING

DEATH FEAST

Another ceremony is the Death Feast. It is a time to remember ancestors.

EUROPEAN CONTACT

Ancestral Seneca first met Europeans in the 1600s. The Seneca became a big part of the fur trade. They were powerful. They defeated other nations to get more furs. They also stopped Europeans from moving farther west.

Conflicts grew in the 1700s. Many Seneca sided with the British during the **Revolutionary War**. The war destroyed many Seneca villages in New York. The Seneca were forced to sign **treaties** after the war. They lost much of their lands. They were forced onto **reservations**.

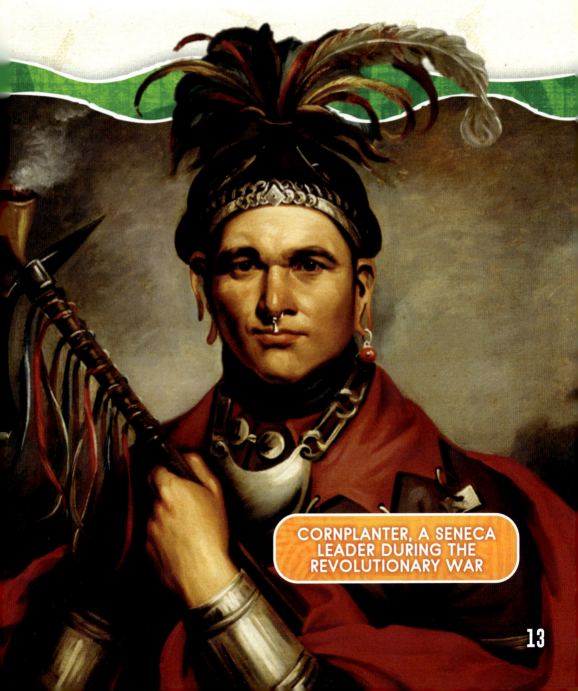

CORNPLANTER, A SENECA LEADER DURING THE REVOLUTIONARY WAR

White people moved farther west in the 1800s. The Indian Removal Act of 1830 forced the Ohio Seneca out from their lands. They were promised lands in Oklahoma in 1831. The path to Oklahoma was hard. Those who survived were met with a broken promise. Part of the land promised to them was also given to the Cherokee Nation.

The Seneca kept fighting for their rights. The Seneca Nation of Indians became federally recognized in 1848. The Tonawanda Band of Seneca soon followed. What is now the Seneca-Cayuga Nation got their reservation lands after years of legal battles in 1902.

FAMOUS SENECA

TANAGHRISSON

BIRTHDAY about 1700

DEATH October 4, 1754

FAMOUS FOR A Seneca leader in the Ohio River Valley who worked to protect his lands from the French

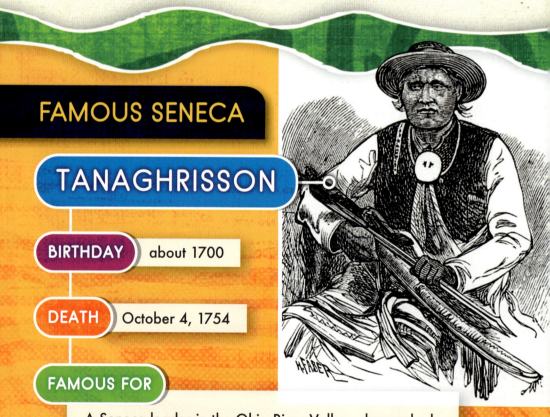

A LAKE NEAR GROVE, OKLAHOMA, THE AREA SENECA PEOPLE WERE FORCED TO AFTER THE INDIAN REMOVAL ACT OF 1830

HAUDENOSAUNEE NATIONS

The Haudenosaunee also includes the Mohawk, Oneida, Onondaga, Cayuga, and Tuscarora nations.

LIFE TODAY

Today, there are three federally recognized Seneca nations. The Seneca Nation of Indians owns five **territories** throughout western New York state. The Tonawanda Band of Seneca's reservation is also in western New York. The Seneca-Cayuga Nation has government **headquarters** in Grove, Oklahoma.

Around 15,000 people identify as Seneca today. Some members live on the nation's lands. Others live throughout the U.S. and in other countries around the world.

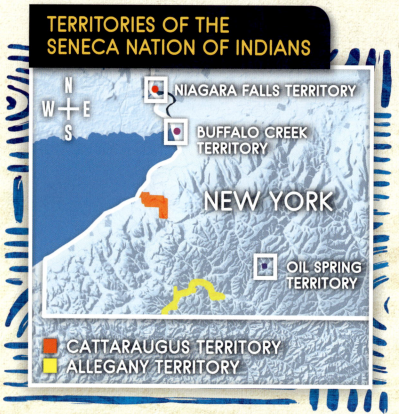

TERRITORIES OF THE SENECA NATION OF INDIANS

SIX NATIONS OF THE GRAND RIVER

The Six Nations of the Grand River is in Canada. This nation includes Seneca and other people with Haudenosaunee backgrounds.

MEMBERS OF THE ALLEGANY SENECA DANCERS

Each of the Seneca nations has its own government. The Seneca Nation of Indians has a president, a **Council**, and courts. The Seneca-Cayuga Nation is led by the General Council. It also has Business and Standing Committees. The Tonawanda Band of Seneca practices a **traditional** government. It is led by chiefs. Clan mothers choose them.

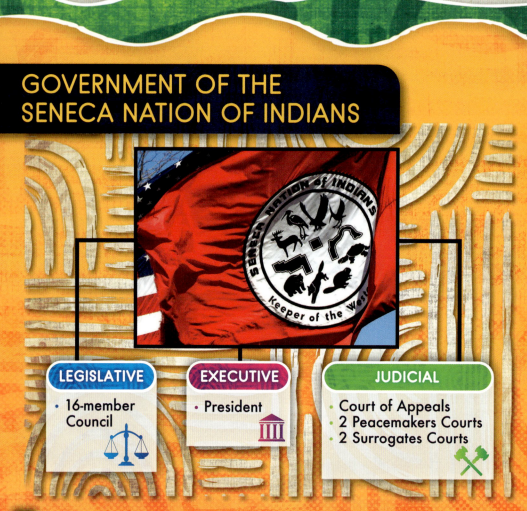

GOVERNMENT OF THE SENECA NATION OF INDIANS

LEGISLATIVE
- 16-member Council

EXECUTIVE
- President

JUDICIAL
- Court of Appeals
- 2 Peacemakers Courts
- 2 Surrogates Courts

SENECA NIAGRA RESORT & CASINO

Each nation provides services to its members. They include education, health services, and more. The nations also run businesses that support their members. The Seneca Nation of Indians and the Seneca-Cayuga Nation run casinos.

CONTINUING TRADITIONS

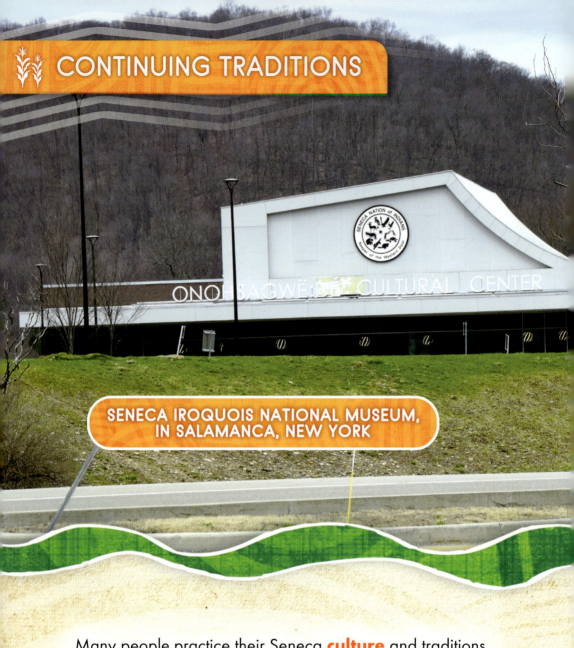

SENECA IROQUOIS NATIONAL MUSEUM, IN SALAMANCA, NEW YORK

Many people practice their Seneca **culture** and traditions. The Faithkeeper's School helps children become confident, independent, and responsible citizens through traditional education. Students learn their ancestors' language. They practice traditions such as sap boiling. The school's farm helps students connect to their culture. They also learn healthy life practices.

DISPLAY AT THE SENECA-IROQUOIS NATIONAL MUSEUM

The Seneca-Iroquois National Museum welcomes visitors to learn about Seneca history and culture. Displays highlight the Creation Story and traditionally made items. The museum also hosts events such as beading and language classes.

HAUDENOSAUNEE MEN'S NATIONAL LACROSSE TEAM

The Seneca-Cayuga Cultural and Historical **Preservation** Program has many programs that honor Seneca traditions. The Culture Summer Camp teaches children crafts, games, and tribal history. They can also play lacrosse games with neighboring tribal nation youth programs!

The Seneca Nation hosts the Marvin "Joe" Curry Veterans **Pow Wow** each July. It is held at the Seneca Allegany Resort & Casino. The event brings different nations together to celebrate their cultures. It has dance contests, crafts, and more.

LACROSSE

Lacrosse is an ancient Haudenosaunee sport. Today, the Haudenosaunee Nationals Lacrosse Organization has men's and women's lacrosse teams. They play lacrosse all around the world!

LACROSSE GEAR

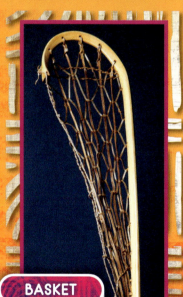

BASKET
has 5 hide strings that represent the five tribal affiliations

BALLS
hardwood burls or animal fur stuffed inside a deerskin cover

STICKS
made from hickory

FIGHT TODAY, BRIGHT TOMORROW

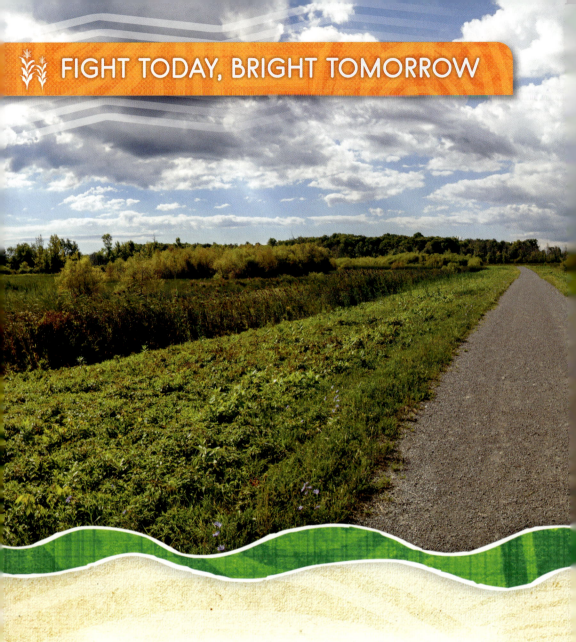

The Seneca have fought for their land rights for hundreds of years. Their fight continues today. The Tonawanda Band of Seneca is facing pressure to let an **industrial park** and pipeline be built next to their land. State officials have kept important information from the nation. They have gone against laws that keep the land safe to pass permits for the park.

24

IROQUOIS NATIONAL WILDLIFE REFUGE

The industrial park could **pollute** the land. It would harm plants that many people use for food and medicine. The nation and its supporters have **protested** to stop the park from being built.

The Seneca Nation fights for their land and **heritage** through a movement called "Stand With Seneca." It shares how the Nation helps Western New York. One of the largest ways the Nation helps the area is by creating jobs. The movement also shares the Nation's successes on social media.

"STAND WITH SENECA" WEBSITE

NATIVE PLANTS

The Seneca Nation has a native plant program. Only native plants can be planted in public areas on Seneca lands.

The Seneca Nation works to make sure its members have food to eat. The Nation's farm is growing its own bison herd. It also plants traditional crops, makes maple syrup, and more. The Seneca are strengthening their future through culture and tradition!

TIMELINE

1142
The Great Law of Peace is created, establishing the Five Tribes of the Haudenosaunee Confederacy

1797
The Treaty of Big Tree is signed, forcing the Seneca to give up much of their lands

1857
The Tonawanda Band separates from the Seneca Nation of Indians to continue a more traditional way of life

1770s
The Seneca are pressured into siding with the British during the Revolutionary War

1848
The Seneca Nation of Indians establishes their own democratic government

1902
What is now known as the Seneca-Cayuga Nation receives reservation lands in Oklahoma

2002
The Seneca Nation of Indians enters into a Gaming Compact with the State of New York

2022
The Seneca Nation of Indians creates the "Stand With Seneca" movement to promote the Nation's positive impact on Western New York

1960s
U.S. officials set Seneca homes on fire and destroy forests in the Allegany Territory after the Kinzua Dam floods nearly 16 square miles (41 square kilometers) of the Allegany Territory

2007
Seneca Buffalo Creek Casino opens in Buffalo, New York

29

GLOSSARY

ancestral—related to relatives who lived long ago

ceremonies—sets of actions performed in a particular way, often as part of religious or spiritual worship

confederacy—a name for a group of Native American nations, such as the Haudenosaunee or Six Nations

council—a group of people who meet to run a government

culture—the beliefs, arts, and ways of life in a place or society

descendants—people related to a person or group of people who lived at an earlier time

headquarters—a government's main office

heritage—the traditions, achievements, and beliefs that are part of the history of a group of people

industrial park—an area that is created for factories or offices

matrilineal clan—a group of people who share a common ancestor that follows a family line through the mother

pollute—to make an area dirty and not safe for use

Pow Wow—a Native American gathering that usually includes dancing

preservation—the act of keeping something in its original state

protested—spoke out against

reservations—lands set aside by the U.S. government for the forced removal of Native American communities from their original lands

Revolutionary War—the war from 1775 to 1783 in which the United States fought for independence from Great Britain

territories—areas of land under the control of a government

traditional—related to customs, ideas, or beliefs handed down from one generation to the next

treaties—official agreements between two groups

TO LEARN MORE

AT THE LIBRARY

Klepeis, Alicia Z. *New York*. Minneapolis, Minn.: Bellwether Media, 2022.

Marcks, Betty. *The Cherokee*. Minneapolis, Minn.: Bellwether Media, 2024.

Sonneborn, Liz. *The Shawnee*. Minneapolis, Minn.: Bellwether Media, 2024.

ON THE WEB

FACTSURFER

Factsurfer.com gives you a safe, fun way to find more information.

1. Go to www.factsurfer.com.

2. Enter "the Seneca" into the search box and click 🔍.

3. Select your book cover to see a list of related content.

INDEX

ceremonies, 10, 11
councils, 18
culture, 6, 7, 10, 11, 20, 21,
    22, 23, 27
Faithkeeper's School, 20
food, 8, 9, 10, 11, 20, 25, 27
future, 27
government of the Seneca
    Nation of Indians, 18
Haudenosaunee Confederacy,
    4, 5, 15, 17, 22, 23
heritage, 26
history, 4, 5, 6, 7, 8, 9, 10,
    12, 13, 14, 15, 21, 22, 24
homeland, 4, 13, 14, 16, 24,
    25, 26, 27
housing, 6, 7
Indian Removal Act of 1830,
    14, 15
lacrosse, 22, 23
language, 20, 21
map, 4, 16
Marvin "Joe" Curry Veterans
    Pow Wow, 22
matrilineal clan system,
    6, 7, 18
members, 16, 17, 19, 27
name, 4

reservations, 13, 14, 16
Revolutionary War, 13
Seneca Nation of Indians, 14,
    16, 18, 19, 22, 26, 27
Seneca resources, 9
Seneca-Cayuga Cultural
    and Historical Preservation
    Program, 22
Seneca-Cayuga Nation,
    14, 16, 18, 19
Seneca-Iroquois National
    Museum, 20, 21
Six Nations of the Grand
    River, 17
"Stand with Seneca," 26
Tanaghrisson, 14
timeline, 28–29
Tonawanda Band of Seneca,
    14, 16, 18, 24, 25
traditions, 6, 7, 10, 11, 18,
    20, 21, 22, 23, 27
treaties, 13

The images in this book are reproduced through the courtesy of: Highsmith, Carol M./ Library of Congress, front cover; Smithsonian American Art Museum/ Wikipedia, p. 3; PaulMassiePhoto, pp. 4-5; unknown/ Wikipedia, p. 5; Alex Hamer/ Alamy Stock Photo, p. 6; Philip Scalia/ Alamy Stock Photo, p. 7; The Book Worm/ Alamy Stock Photo, p. 8; Svetlana Zhukova, p. 9; leopictures, p. 9 (corn); Pavel Kobysh, p. 9 (beans); photofriend, p. 9 (squash); Amelia Martin, p. 10; Studio Light & Shade, pp. 10-11; Janet Rymal, p. 12; Frederick Bartoli/ Wikipedia, p. 13; Ivy Close Images/ Alamy Stock Photo, p. 14; Randall Nyhof/ Alamy Stock Photo, p. 15; J. Passepartout/ Wikipedia, pp. 16-17; Don Heupel/ AP Images, p. 18; JHVEPhoto, pp. 19, 29 (2007); Nosferattus/ Wikipedia, p. 20; Charles/ Flickr, pp. 20-21; ZUMA Press, Inc./ Alamy Stock Photo, p. 22; Carlos Osorio/ Getty Images, p. 23 (all); Eric Dale/ Alamy Stock Photo, pp. 24-25; Singha Songsak P., p. 26; Danita Delimont/ Alamy Stock Photo, p. 27; Dougtone/ Wikipedia, p. 28 (1979); Aozora, p. 29 (2022); Jim Vallee, pp. 28-29; Nativestock.com/ Marilyn Angel Wynn/ Alamy Stock Photo, p. 31.